A POETIC CONFESSION

HEATHER TANTI

Copyright © Heather Tanti 2020

All rights reserved. No part of this book may be reproduced in any form on by an electronic or mechanical means, including information storage and retrieval systems, without permission in writing from the author, except by a reviewer who may quote brief passages in a review.

ACKNOWLEDGEMENTS

To my daughter, thank you for always being my light in the dark.

TABLE OF CONTENTS

Walk Away 9
Broken Glass 11
What For? 13
Petals 15
Self 17
Depression 19
Steel 21
Worth 23
She 25
The Best Parts of Me 27
Take Me As I Am 29
Scars 31
Unreturned Love 33
Warrior 35
Free 37
Time 39
Prey 41
Puppet 43
Who I Was 45
Prisoner 47
Emotions 49
Poison 51
Edges 53
Fragile Mess 55
About the Author 57

HEATHER TANTI

WALK AWAY

Let me go once again,
I'll close my eyes and count to ten.
It'll be as if you were never here, I promise I won't
Shed a tear.
I'll close the door and walk away,
Won't look back,
I'll be okay.
Always leaving,
When times get rough,
It's clear now,
I was never enough.

HEATHER TANTI

BROKEN GLASS

The hurt is real,
It's everything I feel.
The pain is raw,
Like the edges of a saw.
You tear me down,
Like it's a game,
Then turn on me,
Like I'm to blame.
I'm walking on broken glass,
Weaving through,
Like it's a class.
My body's bruised,
My skin is bare,
Wincing as you grab my hair.
You whisper in my ear,
How you can smell my fear.

HEATHER TANTI

WHAT FOR?

Muddy water,
On the ground.
Which way's lost?
Which way's found?

I can't look up,
I can't look down,
The memories,
They follow me around.

I am one,
And I am me.
I am anything but free.
My chains are invisible,
My words are no more.
All this hurting,
But what for?

HEATHER TANTI

PETALS

Petals fall,
Slowly down,
Like silent footsteps,
On the ground.
One by one,
They lose their way,
Drifting into another day.
Their colour fades,
Like many before,
Blowing past your open door.

HEATHER TANTI

SELF

Help me see the truth in me.
I'm slowly forgetting,
Who I used to be.

I'm just an empty vessel now,
Something from,
The lost and found.

A shiny object,
On a shelf,
A whisper of her former self.

HEATHER TANTI

DEPRESSION

Depression is a scary thing,
It takes away your reason
To sing.
It creeps in to eat you alive,
Damages your soul,
And ability to thrive.
It doesn't care how much you try,
It takes pleasure,
In watching you cry.
Depression can be a lifelong curse,
Twisting your mind,
And making it worse.
You take a pill,
To clear the sound,
And prepare to battle,
One more round.
You try to remember,
The blessings in sight,
And hold onto that feeling,
With all your might.

Heather Tanti

STEEL

I see you standing there,
The wind in your hair.
The feeling of freedom,
That used to be there.
Can you feel it?
The tension leave your soul?
Can you feel yourself,
Lose all control?
Don't hide from the light,
That makes you who you are.
Don't forget your struggles,
And how you've come this far.
The brokenness inside,
Will slowly begin to heal.
You'll come out stronger,
You're made of steel.

HEATHER TANTI

WORTH

I see the hurt in your eyes,
I see through your disguise.
You aren't fooling anyone,
With those lies.

Darling, what is your worth?
You've been kicked to the dirt.
With trembling knees,
You continue to please,
Because it's all you know how to do.

Stop selling yourself short,
Like every time before.
Climb to your feet,
Refuse to be beat.

You're worth so much more,
Then you've been fighting for.

Heather Tanti

SHE

She loves you so much,
Can't you see?
She'd do anything,
Just set her free.
She's selfless and fragile,
She's been through hell.
She's been broken and beaten,
From the moment she fell.
Her sleep is uneasy,
Days are a blur.
She's waiting for the miracle,
You promised to occur.
Love her gently,
Love her true.
For her heart is shattered,
And repaired with glue.
Her scars are present,
But she still believes,
That forever exists,
In the lies you weave.

THE BEST PARTS OF ME

God bless this beautiful mess,
And the aching since you left.
I know I'm gonna be okay,
Just get through another day.

You have a way of changing me,
Until I'm losing the best parts
That you never cared to see.

I don't know what this life holds,
But it gets better,
I've been told.
Honestly, I'm a wreck,
If you bothered to check.

I'm going to hold my own heart,
You'll see,
Because it carries the best parts
Of me.

Heather Tanti

TAKE ME AS I AM

You take me down a notch or two,
Every day,
It's something new.
Will I ever be enough?
Or should I call your bluff?

So much love in my heart,
And it was yours,
From the start.
I battle for your time,
Standing in your endless line.

Love me for me,
And the imperfections you see.
Stop trying to change who I am,
I know your love,
Is just a scam.

I deserve love and appreciation,
Not this heartbreaking sensation.
Take me as I am,
Or let me go.
A relationship takes more,
Then this one man show.

HEATHER TANTI

SCARS

Her skin is pale,
Against the light.
The mirror reveals,
A ghastly sight.
What once was ivory,
Smooth and pure,
Now holds scars that seek a cure.
Covered up with baggy clothes,
Another day that no one knows.
The pain escapes,
In bright red ink,
Swirling down an empty sink.
Always promising,
This will be the last,
Until the next time she's harassed.
The pain is silent,
Yet screams release,
The only time she finds her peace.

HEATHER TANTI

UNRETURNED LOVE

Her soul is tired,
Untethered and weak.
Her tears fall,
With words she can't speak.

Always giving,
The best parts of herself,
While forever being kept,
On his dusty shelf.

Her eyes shimmer,
With the pain that she's in,
But she stays silent,
A battle she won't win.

She remembers to breathe,
In and out.
When all she wants to do,
Is scream and shout.

Compassion and love,
Are what fill her heart,
She thought it was wanted,
But it pushed them apart.

Now she's left broken,
Lost and confused.
She once was a dreamer,
But that dreams been used.

HEATHER TANTI

WARRIOR

Like a warrior,
She stands back up,
Always overcoming,
When tides get rough.

With eyes of beauty,
And tears of love,
She wears her scars,
Like a tattered glove.

Forever a dreamer,
With her heart on her sleeve,
She runs with the wind,
She won't be deceived.

FREE

Her strength unravels,
A loose thread.
Slipping from her fingers,
Until there is none.
She can't go back,
Not this time.
Time ticks faster,
Dread fills her stomach,
Fear sticks to her veins.
Her knees are dirty,
The cellar floor cold.
The hairs on her arms raise,
A chill that will never leave.
Her arms are crossed,
Rubbing warmth into her bones.
Bones that ache.
Throb. Break.
Break at the hands of others.
But not now.
Not anymore.
She closes her eyes,
The cold seeps in.
First pain,
Like fire on ice.
Numbness weaves between her soul,
Until finally,
One last breath.
Peace.
She is free.

TIME

Quiet contemplation.
So quiet you hear the cricket's song.
Your feet brush lightly over blades of green.
You yearn to giggle like a little girl,
Running barefoot through the innocence of life.
You smile.
A smile you haven't smiled in years.
Wind rushes across your cheeks,
Teasing the golden ringlets.
A tangled dance of youth.
You're so close.
Salt from the ocean entwines with the breeze.
Your lungs expand,
Inhaling the scent of childhood summers.
A sharp pain trails quickly behind.
A reminder of time.
Always changing,
Numbering the breaths of life we take.
You close your eyes,
Heaviness on your lids.
Your breaths are already numbered,
Nearly running out.
With your last bit of strength,
You push the pain away.
Returning to that little girl on the beach,
Feeling the gentle breeze touch your skin.
You are no longer afraid.
You float effortlessly into an eternal sleep,
With the taste of salty air on your lips.

PREY

"Don't be afraid",
She whispered to her reflection.
Pulling on her dress,
Preparing for rejection.
She turns in a circle,
Her eyes in mirror view.
She wonders what would happen,
What she would do,
If that boy asked her to dance,
In the middle of the room.
She dreamt of the chance,
But boys can be cruel,
Stoking the fire,
Adding more fuel.
She was the prey,
And they were the captor.
Stealing her innocence,
Killing her laughter.

Heather Tanti

PUPPET

Your voice stands still.
Ringing like an aftershock.
I try to block you out;
You're everywhere.
My head.
My heart.
My every breath.
Like a poison that promises to cure,
I drink you in,
Every taste more intoxicating then the last.
You are my demise,
Yet I can't get enough.
Like an addict needing a fix,
I follow you.
A lost puppet in your shadow.
In this darkness,
I know you are wrong for me.
But I return;
Every time.
For a chance to be part of you,
No matter how dark that may be…

Heather Tanti

WHO I WAS

Let me in.
Into the light.
I can't take this darkness,
Can't win this fight.

Don't let go.
The warmth of your touch,
Spreads through my bones,
My soul in your clutch.

I'm losing my sanity,
With each knife in my back.
Sweet and naïve,
Careening off track.

HEATHER TANTI

PRISONER

Exhaustion.
Deep in her bones.
Spreading like venom,
Sinking like stones.
Impossible to leave her,
A wild flower she can be.
Consumed by so much pain,
She longs to break free.
She's not who she stated,
Much to your surprise.
No longer is she foolish,
Forever more wise.
A prisoner of passion,
A nightmare in disguise,
Believing all your stories,
All the little lies.

EMOTIONS

Truth.
Beautiful, fleeting truth.
Equally craved and hated.
A silent spider weaving in and out of honesty.

Pain.
Endless suffering.
A reminder of living,
While slowly dying.

Silence.
Peaceful, yet deadly.
An invitation of surprise.
A voiceless answer.

Shame.
Soul-shattering.
A battle of the mind.
Forgetting its' mercy,
One step at a time.

Emotions.
Confusing and crazy,
A beautiful mess.
Testing our limits,
And what happens next.

POISON

Help me.
I'm drowning.
Drowning in despair.
Can you see me?
Are you almost there?
I've reached the point,
Of no return,
Time's run out,
It's now your turn.
No longer your victim,
A face in the crowd.
The pain of innocence,
That spoke too loud.
Freedom at last,
I've waited so long.
Waited for the moment,
That I would be gone.
Gone from your nightmare,
That poisoned my veins.
Released from your prison,
Free from your chains.

EDGES

Touch me slowly.
Caress my shadow with light.
Bathe upon my soul.
Graze the valleys that separate you from me.
Explore each scar with gentle curiosity,
Tracing their edges like the delicate pages of a book.
Promise not to skip over the bad parts,
It's the only way you'll see.
Why I'm the way I am,
Every time that you touch me.

FRAGILE MESS

A broken, fragile mess,
Left with even less.
Less than when she started,
With her heart full of hope.
Now those shattered pieces,
Scatter down the slope.
You said you wouldn't hurt her,
You'd be different than the rest.
But when push came to shove,
You failed the only test.
Her armour is bruised,
From the times she's been used.
No longer damage that glue can fix,
A pain she never could predict.

ABOUT THE AUTHOR

Heather was born in Ottawa, Ontario on January 9, 1990. Her childhood and adult years were spent growing up in Ontario where she discovered her love for writing at the young age of 7. Fast forward many years and Heather has recently published her first Young Adult novel 'The Way He Loved Me', which describes the struggles/escape of a young girl in an abusive relationship. While fiction writing remains Heather's passion, she also greatly enjoys writing poetry, (just ask the drawer full of notebooks!). Heather is already working on her third novel and is looking forward to growing and connecting with her readers.

Made in the USA
Middletown, DE
02 October 2020